INTERNAL ARTS PRIMER

內部藝術教導

Internal Arts Primer

内
部
藝
術
教
導

Sifu Bob

Copyright

Table of Contents

Dedication

To all my many teachers

Grandmaster William C. C. Chen

Grandmaster Liang Tse Tung

Master Chan Bun-Piac[B]

Dr. John P. Painter

Thomas Morgan – asking the questions and challenging the answers.

And the many more

Remember as T.T. always said "you need teachers and you need books" and now maybe videos ... coming soon?

Preface

This is a Golden Flower publication focused on the reader who has heard of the power of the Internal Arts and how the practice can help them with their health or to the martial artist looking for something else to study. Three of the Internal Arts are used with a simple routine to play with and get an understanding of the arts and how they differ.

This volume is not a source where you will study and become a practitioner of any of these arts. You need teachers and books but it is nice to understand what you are getting involved with. The practice should take you only a few days to understand and one may appeal to you. If one does, then the journey is just starting. Look for a teacher while reading books. Ask questions and look at the answers. Most of all have fun and don't injure yourself.

You can go to our website for details but also look in Google. Use judgment in what you read. This is a life's journey!

Sifu Bob
Season of the coming cold

The Magic Three

This volume will be an introduction to the most well-known of the Internal Arts - Tai Chi Chuan, Bagua Zhang and Hsing I.

Internal Arts - what does that mean? A fascinating thought but not readily understood. The term comes to us from the Martial Arts community - yes, people that practice fighting arts. Somewhere, a distinction was made between the internal arts and the external arts and a vague definition was developed that defined each one. Some are also known as hard and soft arts but this term is not as accurate for defining the practices.

As far back as the 17th century and even before, there are writings defining the internal arts and discussing the loss of many of them with time. For this volume, the discussion will be on the three well-known versions although only Tai Chi Chuan is a common term and the other two are mostly only talked about in the martial art community.

A definition of Internal Arts is needed. This is a martial arts system that uses mental imagery in the practice and development to increase the impact of the training. External arts are more focused on strength and exercise to develop skills. There is a lot of cross over between styles - you can see an internal stylist lifting weights and an external stylist thinking about their movements.

One of the benefits of the internal styles comes from the health benefits of the practices. Since the styles are less impacting on the player, the infirm and unhealthy can practice the arts and benefit from that practice. Relaxed movements and deep, slow breathing help the body heal itself. Movements extend the muscles and expand the joints allowing the flow of the body fluids. Blood pressure is lowered with relaxation.

Each of these arts has a defined feel to them. Tai Chi Chuan is known as the willow leaf fluttering in the wind. Bagua Chuan is the steel leaf spring ready to return the energy back to its source. Hsing I is a steel rod penetrating to its depth. Each of these metaphors provides an image of the art when practicing. Each will be explained in their individual sections. All have references back to the principles of the Yin and Yang and 5 element theories.

Tai Chi Chuan

Tai Chi Chuan is translated as supreme ultimate fist or in some instances long boxing for its continuous movements. It is an ancient martial art. The complete history would require its own book and they are available. It comes from ancient China and is considered an excellent martial art but early in the 19th century one of the great grandmasters understood that it was a valuable tool to heal the sick and decided that Tai Chi[1] needed to be taught to the masses. Some changes were made to alter the martial components and people began to practice throughout the country. Now, it is hard to find someone who knows the martial practices mostly you will find Tai Chi only taught – a form that is most effective for healing people but with no martial applications.

What is provided below is one of the basic and most important movements of Tai Chi. Practicing this will provide you with health benefits but for full benefits of the art, you need to progress to complete forms and the foundation exercises of this and the other two arts discussed in this volume.

Tai Chi Chuan's basic exercise is a number of movements connected together into a set that creates a form. Forms have been many different lengths of movements from small sets up to large sets of 150 or more movements. The emphasis in a number of sets consisting of a lesser amount of movements has come about due to competitions and available practice time have become issues. The original forms were all 100 plus movements using connectors and transition movements to make the form move smoothly. The most common element is called Grasp Sparrow's tale. This will be the focus of this section for discussion, demonstration and practice.

The basic movements of Grasp Sparrow's tail are in this practice session consisting of the movements of ward off, roll back, press and push. This is not a form but an exercise routine to practice and learn the basics. If you give up learning the rest of the art you can continue practicing this set since it contains the major movements of the art. The right side is performed and a transition movement allows the change to the left side. The form can then be returned to the finishing position or if the player wishes the right side can be repeated with the player moving back and for practicing these movements.

Tai Chi Practice Set

Beginning posture
Hold the ball
Ward of left side
Ward of right side
Roll back
Press
Push
Single Whip
Ward off left side
Roll back
Press
Push
Single Whip
Closing

Explanation of the Postures

Beginning Posture

Start with the basic standing posture as discussed earlier. The breath is released and there is a slight bend at the Kua forward. This shifts the weight to the forward part of the foot. The fingers energize and the hands raise up directly in front of the body until at a position with the palms facing down and the hands at shoulder height. The elbows release and the wrists break as the hands move towards the chest. When the elbows are fully bent the wrists straighten and the fingers open palms facing away from the body. The hands then proceed to move down in front of the body until the arms are straightened but not stiff.

Fair Lady's Wrist

Fair Lady's Wrist is a very important part of all the following exercises. Too much and the energy is shut off from flowing into the hands. Too limp and not enough energy is being expressed into the hands. When the wrist is straight and in alignment with the arm and the hand the energy flows as required upon the demand of the player.

1 *Too much bend*

2 *Not Enough Energy*

3 *Fair Lady's Wrist*

4 Hands raise from the fingers

5 Fingers Energize

6 Hands lower and fingers relax

Hold the Ball

The right foot turns of the heel to the right. The weight of the body is shifted to the right foot. The right hand arcing upward to shoulder height palm down and the left hand moving across the waist ending directly under the right palm left palm face up as if holding a ball on the right side of the body.

7 *Hold the ball left*

8 *Hold the ball right*

Ward of left side

The waist turns to the Northeast corner as the left foot is raised slightly off the floor and steps directly ahead with the heel touching down first three or four inches forward of the right foot. The weight shifts to the left foot. The left arm moves in an arch up to shoulder height as the right-hand moves down to the right corner waist. The forearm is level with the palm facing the body in front of the breastbone.

9 *Stepping forward*

1 0 Ward Off Left

Ward of right side

The left hand comes back towards the body as the right hand scoops under in an arc to take a place where both palms face towards each other. The posture looks again like holding a beach ball. The right foot is lifted and steps to the right toe pointing east put the heel down where the toe was. The body turns to the right with the right arm moving in an arc to a position at shoulder level facing east. The left hand stays level and follows the right arm staying a few inches from the arm just behind the right wrist palm facing the right arm.

11 *Stepping Forward*

12 *Ward off Right*

Roll back

Turn the waist to the right with the right arm stretching out while maintaining a 45-degree angle following the waist to the right. The left hand comes in towards the right elbow with the fingertips pointing at the elbow palm facing the body. Shift the weight back to the left leg and then turn the body to the left. The right arm moves in a downward arch and the left hand maintains a location at the elbow. Stop when the right arm is 15 degrees above level.

1 3 Roll back 1

1 4 Roll back 2

1 5 Roll back 3

Press

The left arm moves in a vertical circle coming to meet the right arm at the wrist with the palm of the left hand supporting the right wrist. As this is happening, shift the weight back to the right foot as the arms press forward.

16 *Press 1*

17 *Press 2*

Push

Separate the arms with the palms pointing to the east and moving out to shoulder distance apart as the weight shifts back to the left foot. Shift the weight forward as the arms drop down with the elbows coming close to the ribs. Once the weight is fully forward, push with both palms to the east.

18 *Push1*

19 *Push 2*

2 0 *Push 3*

2 1 *Push 4*

Single Whip

This movement uses only half of the single whip movement to provide for a transition movement from one direction to the opposite. It will be used in the same manner in this set and the next.

The weight is shifted to the left foot with the hands remaining at the current position palms turning to point downward. The arms extend with the rearward movement.[2] When the weight is transferred swing the body to the north continuing to the west as far as is comfortable with the arms following across the horizon. The right foot turns with the body to end at a 45-degree angle towards the North at the end of this movement as the weight shifts back to the right foot.

2 2 Single Whip

Ward off left side

Drop the left arm down to the waist holding the ball with both hands right on top left on bottom and step to the left with the left toe pointing west keeping a shoulder width on the step. Shift the weight to the left leg and the left arm arcs up to a left ward off posture. The left arm is level at shoulder height. The right hand is palm facing to the rear at the right hip.

2 3 *Step Forward*

2 4 *Ward off Left*

The next three movements are identical to the right side. Details will be added with the change of hands.

Roll back

Turn the waist to the left with the left arm stretching out while moving to a 45-degree angle following the waist to the left. The right hand comes in towards the left elbow with the fingertips pointing at the elbow palm facing the body. Shift the weight back to the right leg and then turn the body to the right. The left arm moves in a downward arch and the right hand maintains a location near the elbow. Stop when the left arm is 15 degrees below level.

2 5 Roll back left 1

2 6 Roll back left 2

Press

The right arm moves in a vertical circle coming to meet the left arm at the wrist with the palm of the right hand supporting the left wrist. As this is happening, shift the weight back to the left foot as the arms press forward.

2 7 Press Left 1

2 8 Press Left 2

Push

Separate the arms with the palms pointing to the west and moving out to a shoulder distance apart as the weight shifts back to the right foot. Shift the weight back to the left foot as the arms drop down with the elbows coming close to the ribs. Once the weight is fully forward, push with both palms to the west.

29 *Push left 1*

30 *Push left 2*

3 1 *Push Left 3*

Single Whip

The weight is again shifted back to the right foot with the hands remaining at the current position palms turning to face downward. The arms extend with the rearward movement. When the weight is transferred to the right foot swing the body to the north with the arms following across the horizon and the left foot turning to the north.

3 2 Single whip left

Separate Hands

The beginning of the closing movement has the hands moving in a slight arc up and out to the sides until the arms are at the sides of the body extended elbows down slightly and hands open. As the arms move the right foot is pivoted to the north so both feet are parallel to the north.

3 3 Separate Hands 1

Cross Hands

The hands continue to move in the arc circling down and crossing at the waist right hand on the outside. The hands continue up to chest height and stop.

3 4 Cross Hand 1

3 5 Cross Hands 2

Closing

The hands then drop uncrossing the arms as the hands come to the side with the palms facing towards the back. This ends the form.

3 6 *Wu Chi*

Repetitions

Repetitions for this set can be completed by eliminating the closing part of the set and going from side to side with the single whip transition. The second single whip continues and completes into the right ward off movement. This will allow for the repetition of both sides until the player decides to finish the exercise. Continue the turn until facing the corner. The right hand drops down to hold the ball facing North East with the left hand at the top. The right hand circles upward to a ward off position and the left hand drops to the left hip palm facing back. The player then goes into roll back, press and push and then turns to the other side to continue the form.

Tai Chi Practice Set 2

This second set uses the same techniques as in the first practice set but adds an extra Ward off to allow the additional movement allowing the player to move to all four corners of the compass. The list of movements is below and the explanation follows the listing.

List of Postures in Set 2

Section 1

Beginning posture - North
Hold the ball -   North East
Ward of left side - North
Ward of right side - East
Roll back - East
Press – East
Push – East
Single Whip - West

Section 2

Ward off left side - West
Ward off right side - North
Roll back -   North
Press - North
Push - North
Single Whip - West

Section 3

Ward of left side - South
Ward of right side – West
Roll back - West
Press - West
Push - West
Single Whip - South

Section 4

Ward off left side - East
Ward off right side - South
Roll back - South
Press - South
Push - South
Single Whip - East
Separate Hands - North
Closing – North

The first section of this second set is the same as in the movements of the first exercise but when the movement of the single whip takes the player to the west the next movement is a left ward off followed by a right ward off to the north. Then the movements of the Grasp Sparrow's Tail are followed facing the north (section 2) rather than the west as in the first practice. The single whip movement takes the player to the south (section 3) and ward off left followed by ward off right takes the player to the west. Again the transition movement of single whip changes the direction to the east and the ward off takes the movements to the south (Section 4). A closing movement of separate hands allows the player to go back to their starting position. Since this is an introduction to Tai Chi Chuan, this is a complex set but with practice, it becomes something you can play with and develop many of the art's finer movements. This is for only the right side of the form and the whole set can be performed as a left-sided set but that is for a more dedicated volume.

Second Set Tai Chi Chuan Exercise

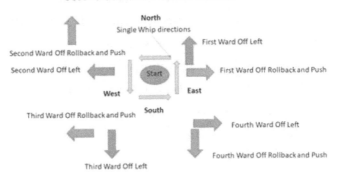

A graphic below gives the direction that the single whip movement will go to get into the next ward off movement except for the fourth one which goes into separate hands and closing movements described below.

Single whip rotation

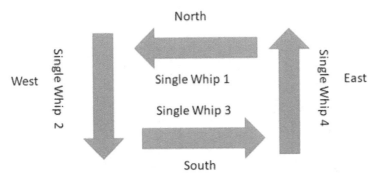

The descriptions below are the same as in the first exercise. Pictures have not been duplicated except where necessary to explain the movement or a transition.

Second Practice Set - Postures

Beginning Posture

Start with the basic standing posture as discussed earlier. The breath is released and there is a slight bend at the Kua forward. This shifts the weight to the forward part of the foot. The fingers energize and the hands raise up directly in front of the body until at a position with the palms facing down and the hands at shoulder height. The elbows release and the wrists break as the hands move towards the chest. When the elbows are fully bent the wrists straighten and the fingers open palms facing away from the body. The hands then proceed to move down in front of the body until the arms are straightened but not stiff.

3 7 *Starting posture 1*

3 8 *Starting Posture 2*

39 *Starting Posture 3*

40 *Starting Posture 4*

4 1 Starting Posture 5

Hold the Ball

The right foot turns of the heel to the right. The weight of the body is shifted to the right foot. The right hand arcing upward to shoulder height palm down and the left hand moving across the waist ending directly under the right palm left palm face up as if holding a ball on the right side of the body.

4 2 *Hold the ball Left*

First Section

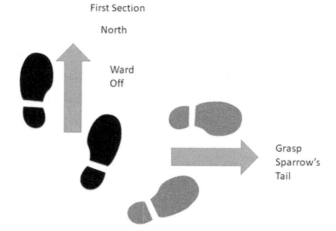

First Section

North

Ward
Off

Grasp
Sparrow's
Tail

The waist turns to the Northeast corner as the left foot is raised slightly off the floor and steps directly ahead with the heel touching down first three or four inches forward of the right foot. The weight shifts to the left foot. The left arm moves in an arch up to shoulder height as the right hand moves down to the right corner waist. The forearm is level with the palm facing the body in front of the breastbone.

Foot positions in Ward off changes

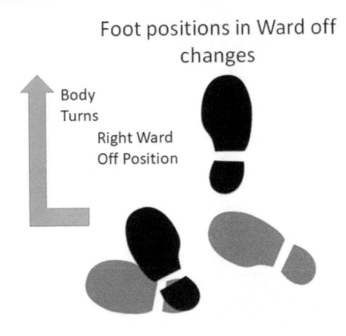

Body
Turns

Right Ward
Off Position

Left Ward Off
Position

As seen above the right foot steps to the toe and a 90-degree angle from its previous position and when the weight is shifted to the right foot the left foot pivots on the heel to the same direction slightly off between 30 and 45 degrees.

4 3 Stepping

4 4 Ward Off Left

Ward of right side

The left hand comes back towards the body as the right hand scoops under in an arc to take a place where both palms face towards each other. The posture looks again like holding a beach ball. The right foot is lifted and steps to the right toe pointing east put the heel down where the toe was. The body turns to the right with the right arm moving in an arc to a position at shoulder level facing east. The left hand stays level and follows the right arm staying a few inches from the arm just behind the right wrist palm facing the right arm.

4 5 Stepping   4 6 Ward Off Right

Roll back

Turn the waist to the right with the right arm stretching out while maintaining a 45-degree angle following the waist to the right. The left hand comes in towards the right elbow with the fingertips pointing at the elbow palm facing the body. Shift the weight back to the left leg and then turn the body to the left. The right arm moves in a downward arch and the left hand maintains a location at the elbow. Stop when the right arm is 15 degrees above level.

4 7 Roll back 1

4 8 Roll back 2

Press

The left arm moves in a vertical circle coming to meet the right arm at the wrist with the palm of the left hand supporting the right wrist. As this is happening, shift the weight back to the right foot as the arms press forward.

4 9 Press 1

5 0 Press 2

Push

Separate the arms with the palms pointing to the east and moving out to shoulder distance apart as the weight shifts back to the left foot. Shift the weight forward as the arms drop down with the elbows coming close to the ribs. Once the weight is fully forward, push with both palms to the east.

5 1 Push 1   5 2 Push 2

5 3 *Push 3*

5 4 *Push 4*

Single Whip

This movement uses only half of the single whip movement. The weight is again shifted back to the left foot with the hands remaining at the current position palms shifting to point downward. The arms extend with the rearward movement. When the weight is transferred swing the body to the north continuing to the west as far as is comfortable with the arms following across the horizon. The right foot turns with the body to end at a 45-degree angle at the end of this movement as the weight shifts back to the right foot.

Repetitions and directions

From this point on the form is repetitious moving to cover front, back, and both sides. The movements are the same but at the beginning, the player will experience confusion in which way to move. This is a good thing since it will challenge the brain and ingrain into the body the movements. Since these are essential movements in Tai Chi Chuan the practice of them is critical to experience growth in the art.

The pictures will not be repeated in the section below but an indication to the direction is included in the diagrams with each section. Printing out the charts and posting them on the wall always helps get the direction into movements ingrained in the body.

Each section will be supplied with a simple diagram that shows the ward off direction and the other movements which are called Grasp Sparrow's Tail in the Tai Chi Chuan form.

Second Section

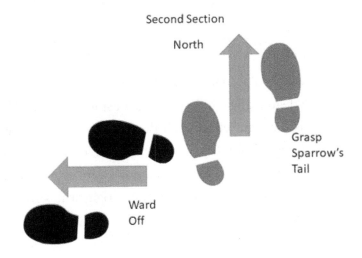

Grasp
Sparrow's
Tail

Ward
Off

Ward of left side

The waist turns to the Northeast corner as the left foot is raised slightly off the floor and steps directly ahead with the heel touching down first three or four inches forward of the right foot. The weight shifts to the left foot. The left arm moves in a circular motion up to shoulder height as the right hand moves down to the right corner waist. The forearm is level with the palm facing the body in front of the breastbone.

Ward of right side

The left hand comes back towards the body as the right hand scoops under in to take a place where both palms face towards each other. The posture looks again like holding a beach ball. The right foot is lifted and steps to the right toe pointing east put the heel down where the toe was. The body turns to the right with the right arm moving in an arc to a position at shoulder level facing east. The left hand stays level and follows the right arm staying a few inches from the arm just behind the right wrist palm facing the right arm.

Roll back

Turn the waist to the right with the right arm stretching out while maintaining a 45-degree angle following the waist to the right. The left hand comes in towards the right elbow with the fingertips pointing at the elbow palm facing the body. Shift the weight back to the left leg and then turn the body to the left. The right arm moves in a downward arch and the left hand maintains a location at the elbow. Stop when the right arm is 15 degrees above level.

Press

The left arm moves in a vertical circle coming to meet the right arm at the wrist with the palm of the left hand supporting the right wrist. As this is happening, shift the weight back to the right foot as the arms press forward.

Push

Separate the arms with the palms pointing to the east and moving out to shoulder distance apart as the weight shifts back to the left foot. Shift the weight forward as the arms drop down with the elbows coming close to the ribs. Once the weight is fully forward, push with both palms to the east.

Single Whip

This movement uses only half of the single whip movement. The weight is again shifted back to the left foot with the hands remaining at the current position palms shifting to point downward. The arms extend with the rearward movement. When the weight is transferred swing the body to the north continuing to the west as far as is comfortable with the arms following across the horizon. The right foot turns with the body to end at a 45-degree angle at the end of this movement as the weight shifts back to the right foot.

Third Section

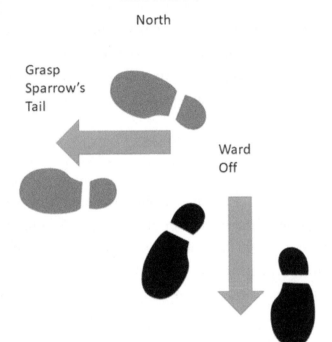

Third Section

North

Grasp Sparrow's Tail

Ward Off

Ward of left side

The waist turns to the East corner as the left foot is raised slightly off the floor and steps directly ahead with the heel touching down first three or four inches forward of the right foot. The weight shifts to the left foot. The left arm moves in an arch up to shoulder height as the right hand moves down to the right corner waist. The forearm is level with the palm facing the body in front of the breastbone.

Ward of right side

The left hand comes back towards the body as the right hand scoops under in an arc to take a place where both palms face towards each other. The posture looks again like holding a beach ball. The right foot is lifted and steps to the right toe pointing east put the heel down where the toe was. The body turns to the right with the right arm moving in an arc to a position at shoulder level facing east. The left hand stays level and follows the right arm staying a few inches from the arm just behind the right wrist palm facing the right arm.

Rollback

Turn the waist to the right with the right arm stretching out while maintaining a 45-degree angle following the waist to the right. The left hand comes in towards the right elbow with the fingertips pointing at the elbow palm facing the body. Shift the weight back to the left leg and then turn the body to the left. The right arm moves in a downward arch and the left hand maintains a location at the elbow. Stop when the right arm is 15 degrees above level.

Press

The left arm moves in a vertical circle coming to meet the right arm at the wrist with the palm of the left hand supporting the right wrist. As this is happening, shift the weight back to the right foot as the arms press forward.

Push

Separate the arms with the palms pointing to the east and moving out to shoulder distance apart as the weight shifts back to the left foot. Shift the weight forward as the arms drop down with the elbows coming close to the ribs. Once the weight is fully forward, push with both palms to the east.

Single Whip

This movement uses only half of the single whip movement. The weight is again shifted back to the left foot with the hands remaining at the current position palms shifting to point downward. The arms extend with the rearward movement. When the weight is transferred swing the body to the north continuing to the west as far as is comfortable with the arms following across the horizon. The right foot turns with the body to end at a 45-degree angle at the end of this movement as the weight shifts back to the right foot.

Fourth Section

Fourth Section

North

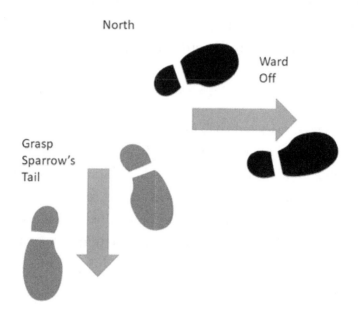

Ward
Off

Grasp
Sparrow's
Tail

Ward of left side

The waist turns to the Southwest corner as the left foot is raised slightly off the floor and steps directly ahead with the heel touching down first three or four inches forward of the right foot. The weight shifts to the left foot. The left arm moves in an arch up to shoulder height as the right hand moves down to the right corner waist. The forearm is level with the palm facing the body in front of the breastbone.

Ward of right side

The left hand comes back towards the body as the right hand scoops under in an arc to take a place where both palms face towards each other. The posture looks again like holding a beach ball. The right foot is lifted and steps to the right toe pointing east put the heel down where the toe was. The body turns to the right with the right arm moving in an arc to a position at shoulder level facing east. The left hand stays level and follows the right arm staying a few inches from the arm just behind the right wrist palm facing the right arm.

Rollback

Turn the waist to the right with the right arm stretching out while maintaining a 45-degree angle following the waist to the right. The left hand comes in towards the right elbow with the fingertips pointing at the elbow palm facing the body. Shift the weight back to the left leg and then turn the body to the left. The right arm moves in a downward arch and the left hand maintains a location at the elbow. Stop when the right arm is 15 degrees above level.

Press

The left arm moves in a vertical circle coming to meet the right arm at the wrist with the palm of the left hand supporting the right wrist. As this is happening, shift the weight back to the right foot as the arms press forward.

Push

Separate the arms with the palms pointing to the east and moving out to shoulder distance apart as the weight shifts back to the left foot. Shift the weight forward as the arms drop down with the elbows coming close to the ribs. Once the weight is fully forward, push with both palms to the east.

Single Whip

This movement uses only half of the single whip movement. The weight is again shifted back to the left foot with the hands remaining at the current position palms shifting to point downward. The arms extend with the rearward movement. When the weight is transferred swing the body to the north continuing to the west as far as is comfortable with the arms following across the horizon. The right foot turns with the body to end at a 45-degree angle at the end of this movement as the weight shifts back to the right foot.

Separate Hands

This is a new movement but only a variation from the first set. Your position will be at the ending of the single whip and the weight is on the right foot. Lift the left foot and place it down facing North. The weight will shift to the left foot as you continue the hands coming to the North arms extended. When the weight is on the left leg turn the right foot parallel to the left foot shoulder width apart. The arms arc upwards and to the sides in a wide downward arc coming together at the waist and raising up to a crossed arm position in front of the body.

5 5 Separate Hands

Closing

The right arm is on the outside. The hands then drop uncrossing the arms as the hands come to the side palms facing towards the back. This ends the form.

5 6 Cross Hands

Tai Chi Chuan Posting

Tai Chi Chuan has a static exercise called by a number of different names but here will be referred to as posting- standing like a post in the ground. When Tai Chi Chuan is seen, it is almost always a group of people doing the form – a series of postures that transform from one into the next just like in the previously described sets. Posting takes one of these movements and the player assumes the position and maintains the posture for a time. Some call this mediation but a better analogy would be yoga since this act is a very involved set of micro movements and mind control to develop the posture to the rules and energies as guided by the Tai Chi Chuan principles.[1] This is a not a well-known aspect of the art but the earliest teachers of the art highlight how important it is to develop the art using this aspect of it.

Posting involves assuming the posture – two of them are directly referenced by these teachers[1] - Stating posture and tree-hugging posture as seen below. Once in the standing posture the player relaxes into the proper form of the posture and adjusts the body to meet the guidelines provided by the teachers. The mind is also focused on the correct movement of energy in the body. A complete description of this process is out of the scope of this volume but can be found in the books provided by Golden Flower Internal Arts but the player can try one of these postures standing for a minute and allowing the body to relax and the mind to focus.

In the meantime, try standing in one of the postures relaxing and concentrating of the body start with a minute and working up to 5 or 10 minutes to see how much benefit you can obtain.

Posting and the other standing methods which are described in each section can all be classified under the umbrella of Zhan Zhuang – a standing meditation practice. A complete volume on this practice can be found at the Sifu Bob Amazon Page.

5 7 Wu Chi

5 8 Tree Hugging Posture

Bagua Zhang

Bagua Zhang, eight (ba) Trigram(gua) palm(Zhang) is an art very ancient based on the Chinese Yin Yang circle and the theories accompanying that circle. Practice is mostly seen as someone walking around the circle with static hand postures. The art is more than that but learning the art of the circle is the basic tenant of the art and provides a vigorous exercise to the player. Once the art of walking the circle is understood there are numerous hand leg and foot movements added making this art very complex but interesting to study.

Bagua uses relaxation but also a built-in tension of the body to generate energy. This makes the player feel as if there is no give to their body but has the ability to send the person flying away. This energy can be focused when walking the circle generating strength and energy to the player improving their health and wellbeing combatting diseases.

Below we will start with walking the circle and then develop a simple posture to provide the player with the feel of the energy of the circle. As you walk around the circle feel as if there is a fountain of energy coming out of the ground in the center of the circle and shooting to the sky. Walking the circle, you are the wiring, circling the shaft of the motor to generate electric and magnetic current.

The two diagrams below show two phases of the I Ching that are the basis of the Bagua practice. Each trigram is an energy with associated palms which change at that location when walking the circle. The theory is quite involved and leads to a detailed understanding of the art and its associated energies. Complete descriptions are in the texts from Golden Flower Internal Arts.

5 9 *Pre Heaven Bagua*

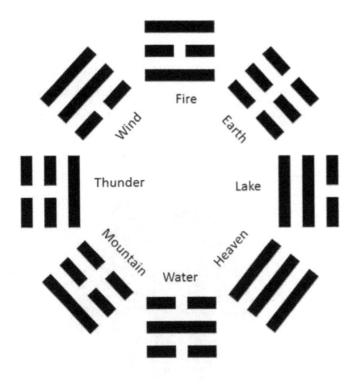

6 0 *Post Heaven Bagua*

Making your Circle

The circle is made to walk. Make your own circle. Put one foot down and step out as far as you can with the other foot and mark that position. Draw a circle at that distance around the center point and then you have your beginning circle.

Center of
Circle

Outside
Edge

***6 1** Creating your Circle*

Ba Posture

The Ba Posture – yes the Ba in Bagua looks like the eight character in Chinese.

Ba – Eight 八

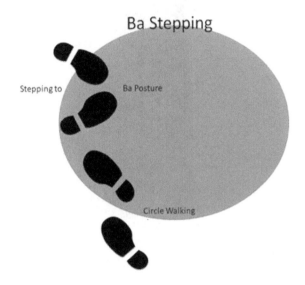

6 2 *Ba Step*

This step provides the ability to turn directions and power into the next step. It is a major stepping technique in Bagua and allows for the change of direction smoothly and provide power out of the step. A full discussion for this step is included in the Bagua Volume and Qigong Volumes.

Circle walking

Walking the circle starts at the center point. Both feet pointing to the top of the circle which should be chosen as the north position. Stand in the normal standing posture. The hands should raise up in a circular movement at the sides of the body meeting just above the head and then moving together to a position at waist level. The hands should be palms down index fingertips pointing at each other separated by a few inches.

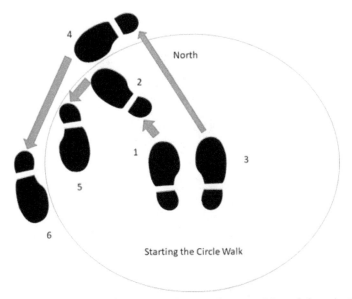

Starting the Circle Walk

Begin with the left foot stepping to the outside of the circle with the foot turning to a 45-degree angle and just to the inside of the drawn line. The weight shifts to the left foot and the right foot is picked up as soon as the weight is transferred. The foot is picked up heel to toe at a height just high enough to pass over the ground and is placed on the outside of the circle pointing in at a 15-degree angle just ahead of the left foot.

The waist is turned at a comfortable angle to the center of the circle. Each foot is picked up by the heel stepping on its side of the circle just a few inches ahead of the previous step. This makes for a slow short deliberate step.

6 3 Starting Posture

6 4 Clearing Posture Yang

6 5 *Clearing Posture Yin*

6 6 *Ready Posture*

6 7 *Double Yin Posture*

6 8 *Heaven's Palm Double Yang Posture Walking*

After walking the circle at least once and returning to the starting point perform a simple turn as described below. During the turn, the hands turn over palms up and slowly raise up to a shoulder height during the turn and the player begins to walk the circle in a clockwise direction in a Yang posture.

The Simple Turn

Walking the circle should be practiced in both a clockwise and a counterclockwise direction. Accomplishing this can be a simple process – a simple turn or a complex movement - a palm change. The simple turn gets you started. Walk the circle for any number of turns until returning to the starting point. The inside foot – in this instance the left foot turns in to a 45-degree angle and the right flowing foot swings with the body into the circle and the toes of the right foot point to the toes of the left foot making a V. While the weight is on the right foot the left foot swing to the outside of the circle and is placed pointing in the opposite direction of the previous movements. The weight transfers to the left leg and the right leg comes up and steps to the inside of the circle. This completes a basic inside turn. The hands during the first turn are maintained in the same location without any extraneous movement. The circle is then walked in the opposite direction.

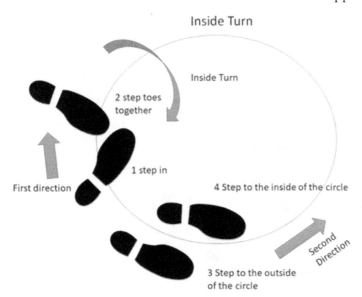

Inside Turn

Walking the circle, you can turn to the outside to change your direction. While walking, the outside foot steps away from the circle 90 degrees. The inside foot swings around and the toe is pointed to the outside foot toe to the side of the opposite toe. The weight is shifted to the foot and the first foot swings back onto the outside of the circle now pointing in the opposite direction. The weight shifts and the back foot comes into the inside of the circle and steps forward.

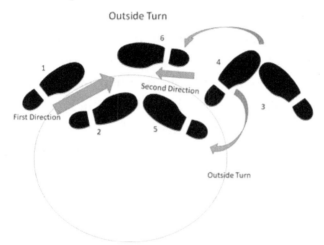

These turns look complicated but practice slowly and the will become natural. Below is another method to practice turns – it is called square stepping. You can practice on the kitchen floor using the tiles as a border.

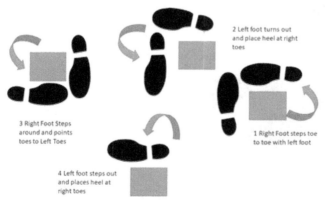

This is the basic circle walking practice. Think of an electric motor and how it generates electricity by spinning around the center conductor. As you become accustomed to the walking you can change you hand postures. A number of options are shown below.

Initial Palms

Walking the circle requires some action with the hands (palms). When beginning walking of the circle a simple set should be used that will be easily maintained until the more advanced hand postures are developed. Do not think that these sets are not valuable since these hand postures are a basic building block of all sets and will be used throughout the advanced forms. Always start at the center of your circle facing North. The hands start at the sides palms facing to the rear and elbows relaxed but slightly away from the body. The hands move away from the sides of the body in an arc and meet slightly higher than the players head a few inches in front of the body. The hands then flow down the center line of the body to the level of the waist. The player then steps out to the edge of the circle with the left foot turning the foot out to the left at a 45-degree angle. The hands form the Yin Heaven Palm – palms down fingers pointing into the other hand maintaining 3 -5 inches apart. The elbows are held away from the body keeping a round feeling to the form. The right foot follows stepping to the outside of the circle as the player begins to walk the circle counter-clockwise.

70 *Twin Yang Palms*

71 *Twin Yin Palms*

7 2 Split posture Top Yang

Single Palm Change

A single palm change incorporates the movement of the upper body into the simple change as described above. The Heaven posture palms will be used in this description to maintain a simple to describe process. This posture is using a split posture with one hand in a Yang Heaven's Position and the other hand in Heaven's Yin position. It is considered split since it is walking with a yin and yang posture. In this instance, the palms maintain the same energy – Heaven but in any posture, the eight energies of the Eight Palms can be combined in either a yin or yang posture. That will be described and demonstrated in the Bagua Volume.

The starting posture is the same as the simple change and the hands start in the same position. The hands go up to head height and then down the front side of the body and come back to the starting position. With the first step of the left foot, the palm of the left hand turns over slowly as the arm creates a circular movement into the center line of the body and starts moving away from the body just below the shoulder level to end up at chin height in a rounded arm posture pointing at the outside line of the circle. The right hand stays palm down moving across the waist to the opposite side of the body and ending palm down just below the left elbow. All these arm actions are with the first left step to the circle. As the right foot comes up to the circle the upper body turns into the circle. This posture is maintained while walking around the circle. This is the Heaven Yang (left) Yin (right) posture.

7 3 Walking counterclockwise

When reaching the top of the circle the simple change is the same for the feet with the left foot turning into the circle and as the right foot comes in to point to the left foot, the Ba posture, the palms remain at the same high / low height but the palms pointing towards each other.

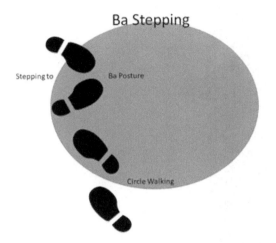

Ba Stepping

7 4 *Facing into circle*

The left foot steps out to the circle as the left arm comes down to shoulder height level to the ground and pushing out palm facing away from the body. The right palm turns palm up pulling back to the right hip.

7 5 *Facing back the previous direction*

The right foot stepping up to the circle brings the right hand under the left elbow wrapping around the body to the ribs. The right hand wipes up the outside of the left arm as both arms raise up. When the right hand reaches the left wrist, the hands separate with the right arm going out and down palm up with the right forward step and the left hand going to the point of the right elbow palm down. The player then continues walking in the opposite direction for the previous rotations.

7 6 Single Palm Change - back view

7 7 Same Movement from the side

Another view of the hand positions in this part of the change. It is important to maintain the energy in the hand as it wraps around the body.

7 8 *Raising the active hand*

The rear foot steps into a Ba stance powering the energy into the hands.

The right wrapping hand slides up the outside of the upper arm whipping across the left arm and then moving out to the ready position as seen below as the left previously raised palm moves down to the right arms elbow. This is performed in the same manner for the opposite side with the appropriate changes in the feet and arms.

7 9 *Assuming the posture*

The palms have completed the change and the circle walk begins with the generic palm position - at this time the palms can assume their respective palm positions and energies.

8 0 *Heaven Palm Yang Yin Posture*

The palms assume their final energy posture – in this instance a Heaven Yang over Heaven Yin.

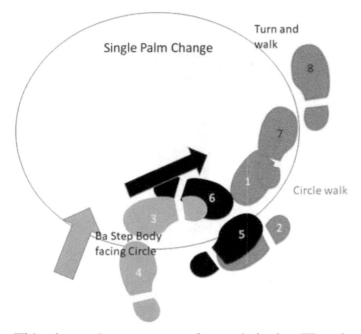

Single Palm Change

Turn and walk

8

7

1

6

Circle walk

3

5

2

Ba Step Body facing Circle

4

This change is not as complex as it looks. The chart preceding this paragraph looks complicated but start with your feet together and then proceed using numbers to make your steps. The initial movement is into the circle and then the movement goes with the arm to the opposite direction (see image 12) then the rear leg steps up as the body turn out away from the circle and then comes back into the circle as the player starts to walk. Do not get discouraged with the first tries to get this right. It takes practice. Later this year (2018) the single change will be on the Golden Flower site as a video.

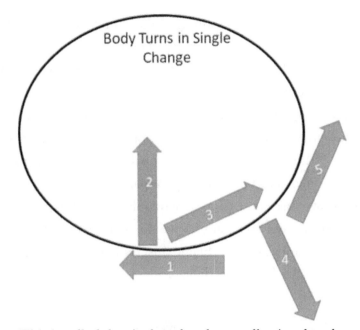

This is called the single palm change allowing the player to walk the circle one direction and make a simple turn with a change in palms to walk the opposite direction. Do not be fooled. This simple move is a large component of this art and has many hidden and seldom explored variations. Walk for a ½ hour and see how much effort it takes. There are a large number of variations in the art of Bagua with, in this instance, the ability to have eight different palms and their Yin and Yang energies. There are a number of posture variations which also adds to the complexity. With the addition of animal postures, the variations in Bagua makes the art endless.

Crossing the Circle

Bagua is most often thought of as only playing in circles but you will find the straight hidden within the circles. This can be found in the simple movement of crossing the circle often called weaving hands. In the normal walking circle, it will be three steps to go from one side to the other passing through the center.

Crossing the circle starts with the beginning of the simple change but the right foot does not stop but steps into the circle. The left foot then follows and the right foot takes the player to the edge of the circle. At this point, you can go either left or right to walk the circle.

An example of this stepping is to use the Heaven Yang Yin palm. As the player steps into the circle and the hands come together the lower hand weaves up the inside of the upper hand with the palm turning from palm down (yin) to palm up (yang). The upper hand turns palm down flowing down to the elbow. This is down three times to pass across the circle. It is a straight movement but is full of circles. You can practice this same movement with any of the palms in Bagua going in a straight line. Just remember the rounded nature of the movements and the energy flow.

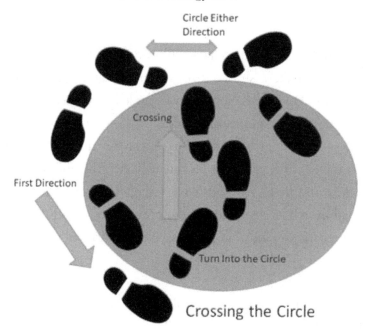

Crossing the Circle

8 1 Weaving Palms1

8 2 Weaving Palms 2

8 3 Weaving palms 3

Bagua Posting

Bagua posting is a practice like that found in both Tai Chi Chuan and Hsing I that uses a static posture to develop the body and mind. Bagua has the tree basic postures as shown below that take the three principles of the Yin and Yang energies and uses those energies in the development practices of the posting. Posting comes from the idea of a post in the ground is rooted and stable. It is the same with the Bagua Posting that the player seeks a strong and rooted position while training the body and mind. The advanced practices use the various palms and stances to develop the energy combining the Yin Yang theory with the 5 elements to create a specific energy. The art of posting is an opening to a magical world with so much potential. A more involved discussion will delve into the art of posting in the Zhang Zhun volume.

8 4 Heavens Yang

8 5 Heavens Yin

8 6 Heaven Split Posture

Hsing I Chuan

Hsing I is an interesting challenge. You will need to take some steps before you can start practicing. So let us begin with the basics. Hsing I is a linear system although it maintains the circles and spirals of the internal arts they are mostly hidden to the beginners. Hsing I fools many people since it does not look like an internal art when practiced. Stomping and fist flying, it looks as if it came directly from a Martial Arts Movie. Before getting there and in good internal practice the art is internal with slow and dedicated movements. The internal aspect of the art has to be developed before the crashing and banging but do not be deterred – it is fun to stomp and punch and there is a great internal value to that part of the art.

Front Step

Assume the standing posture for the Internal Arts. Don't practice in an apartment or other shared building. A nice sandy but firm location is best to start. Shift your weight to the right foot. Step forward with your left foot and stamp down with some energy as you put the foot down heel to toe but with effort. Take the foot back and shift your weight to the left side and step out with the right foot and stamp down. Keep the heel of the forward foot 2 to 3 inches ahead of the toes of the rear foot. Do not bring the feet in line – maintain a shoulder-width distance apart. Also, when you stamp down, start practicing with only a little energy going into the foot. You can increase the power as you practice and gain control of the foot and the energy. Practice this stepping for a few days to allow your foot to get used to the power and weight entering the foot. Be careful, if your foot is not relaxed and in good condition, you can injure the foot even break bones – so slowly and use the energy of your mind.

8 7 *Stepping Forward*

Energy rebound

The stamping of the front foot provides energy going into the foot and the ground. From physics, we know that for every action there is an opposite and equal reaction so feel the energy coming back up the leg. Let this energy flow into your upper body. Be sure that you are not directing it to the lower spine but allowing it to pass through the pelvic girdle[1] into the whole spine and out to the arms and hands. This is good energy that can build up the strength in the upper body but should be generated with care so the body can adjust and accept the energy.

Energy Movement in Drilling Step

Energy flows out the hand

Arm Draws back

Ready position weight on left foot

Step forward with right foot

Energy flow

Stomp

Following Step

After practicing the stomping and filling of the upper body, you can then bring in the following foot. The order is stomping down, energy flowing up to the upper body and then the following step. It is easy to break it down but it is done as one movement when practiced.

The details of the following step start once the front foot is down. The rear foot is unweighted as the weight is transferred to the front foot with the stamp. The rear foot then slides forward and provides a sliding stamp just behind the front foot. This energy is used to energize the rear leg and send energy up it into the body as with the front foot but a microsecond behind. This provides extra force but most importantly does not allow the energy to be misdirected into the rear leg instead forcing all the energy into the upper torso.

8 8 *Left Following Step*

Putting it together

Front Step

Stomp down

Energy flows into the body

Rear step and stomp

Supporting energy flow up the rear leg.

Practicing this can be done using one side stepping keeping the front leg from the same side and moving forward on that leg or Straight Step with the rear foot stepping forward. The rear foot moves up to deliver the energy behind the front foot and then steps forward making it the front foot.

One Sided Straight Stepping

Straight Stepping
Rear leg stepping
Forward

There is also the cross stepping movement that can be seen in one of the pictures below. A foot steps forward but turns in or out at a 45-degree angle and the body is adjusted as the rear foot follows up. The rear foot moves up to take the next step using the same cross stepping movement. The end result is a snake-like path. This is done to practice the action of the feet and the body's follow up. When playing the form, it can be an added part of the form combined with the straight stepping methods.

Crossing stepping in and out

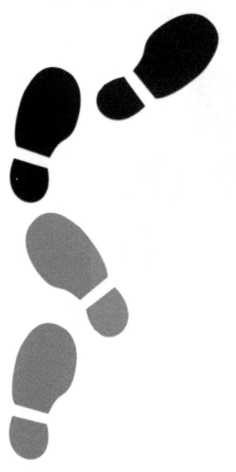

Just move whichever foot is moving forward in a small stepping movement. Hsing I is noted for its small but powerful steps. The crossing step can be each forward step making a snake move across the ground. Using the same foot actually will go into a circle. Once the player is comfortable with the cross step, it can be added to practice and allow the player to wander around the room with in and out stepping.

Oh! The hands!

When first trying to get the feet right don't worry about the hands and arms. Just keep them in front of you, try gripping the hands together. Now, we can bring in what to actually do with the arms and most importantly the hands.

Hsing I has 5 basic hand sets and a large number of animal movements. We are only going to discuss one hand in this exercise called drilling. This is a water exercise so there is not an issue with practicing this and causing injury to the system. More on that in the other volumes.

When starting the form stand in the Internal standing posture. Pull the hands up to the hips creating loose fists palms upward. When stepping forward with the front foot the hand on the side of the foot comes up into the center line and out with the palm of the fist up and the arm circularly extended. The rear hand follows behind the front hand but stops at the front arms elbow. This movement is coordinated with the feet with the end of the hand movement assuming the energy generated from the feet.

The hands will return to the hip location maintaining a loose fist before the next movement. This will create a nice looking practice session. Remember that Hsing I is a martial art. If you are interested in learning the martial components, the hands relax into a posture close to the chest but protecting the center line. Either practice is good for health benefits and beginners. Beginners in forms need to practice with larger form movements to loosen and train the muscles and joints and close up the movements with practice and experience.

8 9 Drilling 1

9 0 Drilling 2

Hsing I Five Forms

The basic five techniques of Hsing I are seen in the pictures below. This volume is an introduction so a complete explanation is too complex and will be covered in the Hsing I volume. Each picture has the basic information so that you can play with a posture but if Hsing I is an art you find near to the heart it must be studied with more reference material presented here.

9 1 Splitting

Splitting is as seen in the picture a chopping action and its element is metal as in an axe.

9 2 *Crossing*

Crossing is of the element of earth. Its springy energy is developed from
the spleen

9 3 *Drilling*

Drilling is of the element of water, and its quality is to fill all gaps.

9 4 *Pounding/blasting*

Pounding is of the element of explosive Fire. Its energy is expressed from the heart

9 5 Crushing

Crushing /crashing technique is like a wooden arrow direct and fast. Its wood energy is from the liver.

Hsing I Animals

Hsing I has 12 animals that are used for movements and energy in the art. The list varies with the style and the teachers. The advanced use of the animal postures investigates the energy movements through the body and the transitions from animal to animal. This can become a lifetime of work to just comprehend the basics of these potentials. Here a list of animals is provided. The Hsing I volume will delve further into the animal sets and energies.

Dragon - heart fire will descend

Tiger - water of the kidneys

Monkey - mind will be stable

Horse - intention coming from the heart

Alligator – dissipate internal heat

Rooster - energy to ascend from the heels

Swallow – exercise the energy in the waist

Hawk - concentrate the energy of the heart

Snake - active aspect within the kidneys

Kestrel -Enliven shoulders and feet

Eagle – Fill the brain and the eyes

Bear - restore your pure passive energy

Hsing I Practice

Hsing I is a somewhat straight art – playing with it takes you on a line sometimes with crooks in it. Playing with Hsing I can present a soft external aspect or a powerful one. Some people can use it to strengthen the body or to relieve stress.

When the player starts to practice, the movements should be slow and deliberate. The energy can be added once the postures are correct. Start playing with the foot movements and then add the hands.

Each Hsing-I Five-Element technique has components which the player learns as they advance in the study. The teaching of the art will develop the stepping and body postures and then advance through the 5 techniques each with it orientation: high, middle, and low.

If you practice work only with one technique until you understand it and can do it flawlessly with all the foot movements. And have fun and play!

Santi

Hsing I is not complete without a reference to the standing and "meditative" posture called Santi. Santi is a static posture that is not static. It is very involved in holding a static position but the body is making micro adjustments and the mind is burning in the correct posture. It is also part of the Internal Arts practice that uses a static posture but the mind and body are developed with the process of holding that posture while correcting the body and concentrating the mind on the body positions. Start with a minute of standing and increase slowly but daily to increase your time standing. Do not over exert one day and forget the next. Standing one minute a day will provide more benefit than standing 1 hour one time a week. Also, a reminder that this is another version of Zhan Zhuang standing art and is covered in the Golden flower book series.

9 6 *Santi a neutral standing position*

The End

It never ends it just takes another breath

This volume has been dedicated to the basic concepts of the Internal Arts. It has focused on the three major styles not negating the quality of other styles but to get an understanding of each of these arts. Once you finish with this volume you can make an informed choice on which art may appeal to you. More reading and investigation is always warranted and then the hard part of finding a good teacher. Remember that this is a lifelong pursuit. There are layers and layers to each of these arts. So much has to be skipped to provide a basic understanding before providing the overwhelming knowledge that goes with each of these systems.

Practice and remember to play. You only will stay with an art if you realize that when the Chinese substitute the word play instead of practice it is for a reason – enjoyment!

The Author

Robert George Downey (Sifu Bob) studied meditation and the martial arts most of his life. He has been a dedicated student of meditation and Internal Arts since 1970. His study started with a wide variety of systems and then focused on the Internal Arts. Sifu Bob has developed an understanding of their associated practices – meditation, qigong, and Traditional Chinese medicine - that leads to increased skills in the arts and improved health. He has studied extensively with Grandmasters Chen and Liang. He has studied and practices Taoist Arts, Tibetan Buddhism, and Zen Meditation. He has been teaching martial arts, meditation, and qigong since the 1980s and is a co-founder of South Shore Internal Arts Association, a martial arts school that has presented seminars in the Internal Arts since the 1970s. Sifu Bob currently runs Golden Flower Internal Arts and writes on Internal Arts subjects and teaches private lessons. His practice includes Tai Chi Chuan and Bagua, meditation and qigong practice, teaching and writing every day.

Goldenflowerinternalarts

Mail

End Notes

[1] Tai Chi – The use of Tai Chi Vs Tai Chi Chuan is to emphasis the use of the art without its martial training.

[2] Extended – At no time is any joint locked in any of the Internal Art's movements. The joint always maintains a level of curvature at the completion of all movements. A locked arm will actually reduce the movement of energy and fluids impeding the flows which lead to a healthier body. See the Daoyin and Qigong volumes for more on this.

[3] Tai Chi Chuan Principles - Tai Chi Chuan has a number of principles established by the early teachers and the principles provide a basis for practicing the art but enough leeway to allow for various interpretations. The 13 principles must execute the mind, chi, and physical movement in one unit. This means that when the mind is focused on a specific area of the body, the chi will flow into that area. When the chi flows into an area, power will follow.

1.   The sinking of Shoulders and Dropping of Elbows

2.   Relaxing of Chest and Rounding of Back

3.   Sinking Chi down to Dan Tien

4.   Lightly Pointing Up the Head

5.   Relaxation of Waist and Hip

6.   Differentiate Between Empty and Full: Yin and Yang

7.   Coordination of Upper and Lower Parts of the Body

8.   Using the Mind Instead of Force

[4] Standing postures teachers – The early public teachers of Tai Chi, Yang Banho and his son Yang Chengfu, make reference to the use of these two postures as critical to learning the art and the need to spend time standing in the form indicating these were the most important postures.

[5] Pelvic Girdle - The body is held together in the middle by a very important structure. It is composed of bones, muscles and connective tissue to allow the upper and lower parts of the body to function independently while still connected. This is the pelvic girdle. It consists of the major muscles groups connecting the back and the legs together in the region of the hips and allows for movement in a circular direction due to the presence of the ball and socket joints of the hips. When connected together by the proper techniques this makes for a stable and powerful structure that also leads to the free flow of energy from the bottom to the top of the body. A complete discussion and breakdown of the parts will be in the Daoyin volume.

Made in the USA
Middletown, DE
31 July 2022

70274817R00066